I Can Read Mu:

a note reading book for CELLO students

by Joanne Martin

Volume 1

© 1991 Summy-Birchard Music
a division of Summy-Birchard, Inc.
Exclusive print rights administered by
Alfred Publishing Co., Inc.
All rights reserved. Printed in USA.

ISBN 0-87487-441-6

The Suzuki name, logo and wheel device
are trademarks of Dr. Shinichi Suzuki used
under exclusive license by Summy-Birchard, Inc.

I CAN READ MUSIC   *CELLO*   Table of Contents

LESSON	C STRING	G STRING	D STRING	A STRING	LESSON	METER	TIME VALUES
1 Pitch			D,E		1 Rhythm	$\frac{2}{4}$	
2 Pitch			D,E		2 Rhythm	$\frac{3}{4}$	
3 Pitch			D,E,F#		3 Rhythm	$\frac{4}{4}$	
4 Pitch			D,E,F#		4 Rhythm	$\frac{5}{4}$	
5 Pitch			D,E,F#		5 Rhythm	$\frac{2}{4}$	
6 Pitch			D,E,F#, G		6 Rhythm	$\frac{3}{4}$	
7 Pitch			D,E,F#, G		7 Rhythm	$\frac{4}{4}$	
8 Pitch			D,E,F#, G		8 Rhythm	$\frac{5}{4}$	
9 Pitch			D,E,F#, G		9 Rhythm	$\frac{2}{4}$	
10 Pitch			D,E,F#, G		10 Rhythm	$\frac{3}{4}$	
11 Pitch			D,E,F#, G	A	11 Rhythm	$\frac{4}{4}$	
12 Pitch			D,E,F#, G	A	12 Rhythm	$\frac{5}{4}$	
13 Pitch			D,E,F#, G	A	13 Rhythm	$\frac{4}{4}$	
14 Pitch			D,E,F#, G	A	14 Rhythm	$\frac{4}{4}$	
15 Pitch			D,E,F#, G	A,B	15 Rhythm	$\frac{2}{4}$	
16 Pitch			D,E,F#, G	A,B	16 Rhythm	$\frac{3}{4}$	
17 Pitch			D,E,F#, G	A,B	17 Rhythm	$\frac{4}{4}$	
18 Pitch			D,E,F#, G	A,B C#	18 Rhythm	$\frac{5}{4}$	
19 Pitch			D,E,F#, G	A,B C#	19 Rhythm	$\frac{3}{4}$	
20 Pitch			D,E,F#, G	A,B C#,D	20 Rhythm	$\frac{4}{4}$	
21 Pitch			D,E,F#, G	A,B C#,D	21 Rhythm	$\frac{3}{4}$	
22 Pitch		G,A			22 Rhythm	$\frac{4}{4}$	
23 Pitch		G,A			23 Rhythm	$\frac{5}{4}$	
24 Pitch		G,A,B			24 Rhythm	$\frac{2}{4}$	
25 Pitch		G,A,B			25 Rhythm	$\frac{3}{4}$	

I CAN READ MUSIC   *CELLO*   Table of Contents

LESSON	C STRING	G STRING	D STRING	A STRING	LESSON	METER	TIME VALUES
26 Pitch		G,A,B,C			26 Rhythm	2/4	*(musical notation)*
27 Pitch		G,A,B,C			27 Rhythm	3/4	*(musical notation)*
28 Pitch		C	D,E,G		28 Rhythm	3/4	*(musical notation)*
29 Pitch		C	D,E,G	A	29 Rhythm	2/4	*(musical notation)*
30 Pitch		B,C	D,E,G	A	30 Rhythm	3/4	*(musical notation)*
31 Pitch		B,C	D,E,F#, G	A,B	31 Rhythm	2/4	*(musical notation)*
32 Pitch		A,B,C	D,E	A	32 Rhythm	3/4	*(musical notation)*
33 Pitch		G,A,B,C	D,E,F#, G		33 Rhythm	3/4	*(musical notation)*
34 Pitch		G,A,B,C	D,E,F#, G	A,B	34 Rhythm	2/4	*(musical notation)*
35 Pitch	C,D				35 Rhythm	2/4	*(musical notation)*
36 Pitch	C,D				36 Rhythm	2/4	*(musical notation)*
37 Pitch	C,D,E				37 Rhythm	3/4	*(musical notation)*
38 Pitch	C,D,E				38 Rhythm	3/4	*(musical notation)*
39 Pitch	C,D,E,F				39 Rhythm	2/4	*(musical notation)*
40 Pitch	C,D,E,F				40 Rhythm	2/4	*(musical notation)*
41 Pitch	F	G,A,C	D		41 Rhythm	2/4	*(musical notation)*
42 Pitch	F	G,A,C	D,E,G		42 Rhythm	3/4	*(musical notation)*
43 Pitch	E,F	G,A,C	D		43 Rhythm	3/4	*(musical notation)*
44 Pitch	E,F	G,A,C	D,E,G		44 Rhythm	2/4	*(musical notation)*
45 Pitch	D,E,F	G,A	D,E	A	45 Rhythm	2/4	*(musical notation)*
46 Pitch	C,D,E,F	G,A,B,C			46 Rhythm	3/4	*(musical notation)*
47 Pitch	C,D,E,F	G,A,B,C	D,E,G		47 Rhythm	6/8	*(musical notation)*
48 Pitch		C	D,E,F,F#, G	A,B,C	48 Rhythm	6/8	*(musical notation)*
49 Pitch		C	D,E,F,F#, G	A,C,D	49 Rhythm	6/8	*(musical notation)*
50 Pitch	C,D,E,F	G,A,B,C	D,E,F,F#, G	A,B,C,C#,D	50 Rhythm	6/8	*(musical notation)*

INTRODUCTION

I Can Read Music is a beginning note-reading book for violoncello students who have learned to play using an aural approach such as the Suzuki Method, or for traditionally taught students who need extra note reading practise. Rhythm and pitch are taught separately, so that the student can work on one thing at a time. When the two aspects of reading are established, they can be combined successfully at a later date.

Before beginning *I Can Read Music* the students should have done some pre-reading work. For pitch reading, students should have a basic understanding of how note names are related to locations on the fingerboard. Teachers and parents should be sure, if they are not already doing so, to refer to notes by name rather than by their location ("address"), i.e., call notes "B" rather than "1 on A". I recommend first teaching the musical alphabet, then using flashcards to teach them the notes in first position (one string at a time). When working with flashcards, the notes should be sung at the correct pitch (use the cello or a piano to establish the pitch). Students who have a well-established pitch memory will learn to read much faster when they relate the written note to the sound in their head. Singing the correct pitch can also develop and refine a student's ear.

Rhythmic preparation should be done as well. Initially I use flashcards with the "Twinkle" rhythms, each quarter-note beat on a card (i.e., four 1/16 notes, or two 1/8 notes, one 1/4 note, etc). A half-note card is twice as wide as a quarter note beat. The rhythms contained in the "Twinkle" theme and variations give a very good foundation for rhythmic reading, and the child can associate the written rhythm with a sound that he or she has already internalized. Initially, I call the rhythms by the names which the students use for the "Twinkle" variations, and talk about quarter notes, eighth notes, etc. after they have learned to clap and play the rhythms.

I Can Read Music is intended to be used at home, with the teacher checking progress at lessons every week or two. Rhythm pages can be clapped first, then played with a steady beat. Pitch pages (at least in the beginning) should be sung at pitch, using their note names, then played. Initially there will be hesitations, but a steady beat should be encouraged.

Throughout most of the book, the pitch pages use 1st, 3rd and 4th fingers. Lessons 48-50 use the 2nd finger as well. On the advice of a number of young musicians, I have used accidentals rather than key signatures. Students will probably need to be told about the rule that an accidental applies to an entire measure. To encourage students to read notes rather than numbers, finger numbers are not used in this book except in the guide at the top of the page when a new pitch is intruduced.

Beginning readers may initially need to have the parent point out the notes to help the child's eyes follow on the page. Experienced readers move their eyes several notes ahead of what they are playing. The parent can help the child learn to read ahead by pointing a note or two past the note being played. The student should be encouraged to play with a steady pulse, and not to go back to fix mistakes. Often a child will need to play a line several times to eliminate hesitations. The parent can help develop rhythmic awareness by counting or tapping a steady beat.

I would like to thank my parents Frances and Kenneth Martin for their continual support and encouragement. I am grateful to Patricia Shand for her wise advice and editing assistance, and to the hundreds of students who have helped me begin to understand learning. *I Can Read Music* is dedicated to my daughter Shauna, who has taught me so much about life, learning, and music.

Joanne Martin

Pitches used in *I Can Read Music (Violoncello)*

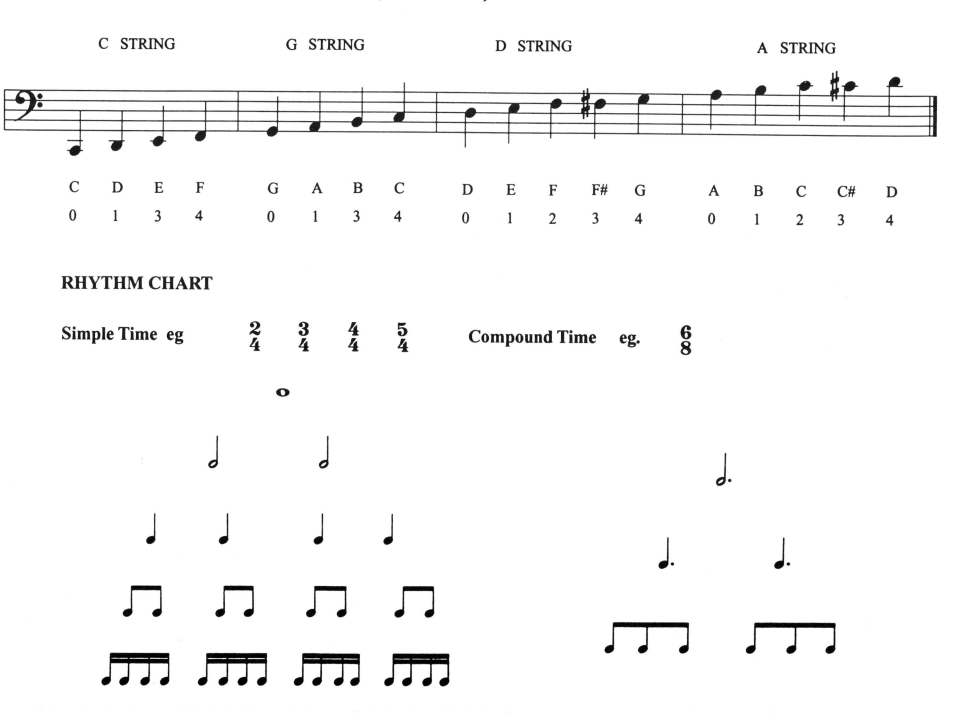

RHYTHM CHART

LESSON 1 - PITCH

LESSON 1 - RHYTHM

LESSON 2 - RHYTHM

LESSON 3 - PITCH

F#
3 on D

LESSON 3 - RHYTHM

LESSON 4 - PITCH

12

LESSON 4 - RHYTHM

LESSON 5 - PITCH

LESSON 5 - RHYTHM

A quarter rest = a silent quarter note

LESSON 6 - PITCH

LESSON 7 - PITCH

LESSON 8 - PITCH

LESSON 9 - PITCH

LESSON 9 - RHYTHM

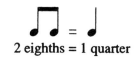

LESSON 11 - PITCH

A
Open

LESSON 12 - PITCH

LESSON 13 - PITCH

30

LESSON 13 - RHYTHM

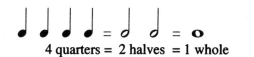

4 quarters = 2 halves = 1 whole

LESSON 14 - PITCH

LESSON 14 - RHYTHM

LESSON 15 - PITCH

LESSON 15 - RHYTHM

LESSON 16 - PITCH

LESSON 16 - RHYTHM

LESSON 17 - PITCH

LESSON 18 - PITCH

LESSON 19 - PITCH

LESSON 19 - RHYTHM

43

LESSON 20 - PITCH

LESSON 20 - RHYTHM

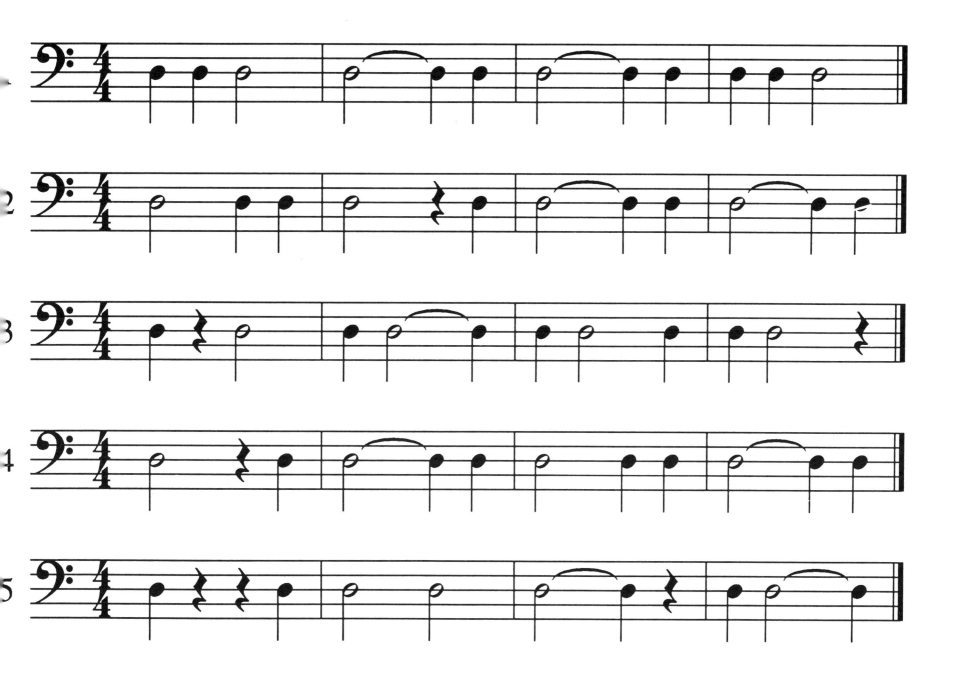

LESSON 21 - PITCH

LESSON 21 - RHYTHM

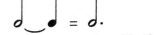

A half tied to a quarter = a dotted half

LESSON 22 - PITCH

LESSON 23 - PITCH

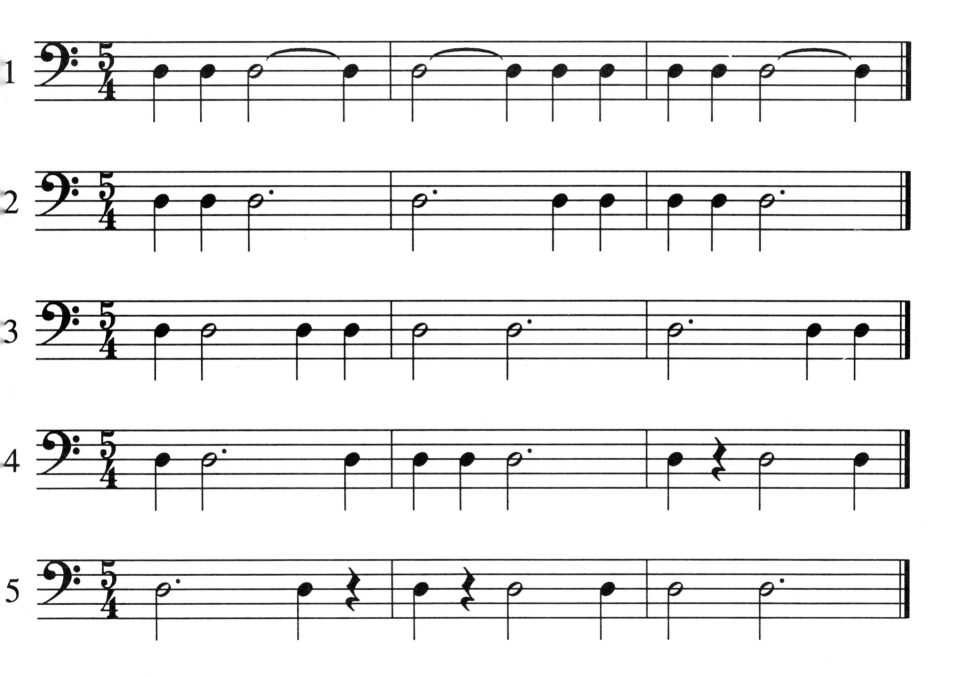

LESSON 24 - PITCH

B
3 on G

1

2

3

4

5

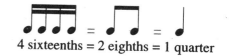

4 sixteenths = 2 eighths = 1 quarter

LESSON 25 - PITCH

56

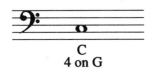

LESSON 26 - PITCH

LESSON 27 - PITCH

LESSON 27 - RHYTHM

LESSON 28 - PITCH

LESSON 29 - PITCH

62

LESSON 29 - RHYTHM

1 eighth and 2 sixteenths = 1 quarter

63

LESSON 31 - PITCH

LESSON 31 - RHYTHM

2 sixteenths and 1 eighth = 1 quarter

LESSON 32 - PITCH

LESSON 33 - PITCH

LESSON 34 - PITCH

LESSON 34 - RHYTHM

An eighth rest = a silent eighth note

LESSON 35 - RHYTHM

LESSON 36 - PITCH

76

LESSON 37 - PITCH

LESSON 38 - PITCH

80

LESSON 39 - PITCH

F
4 on C

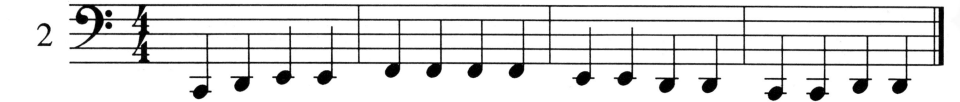

LESSON 40 - PITCH

LESSON 40 - RHYTHM

A quarter tied to an eighth = a dotted quarter

LESSON 41 - PITCH

LESSON 42 - PITCH

LESSON 42 - RHYTHM

LESSON 43 - PITCH

LESSON 44 - PITCH

LESSON 44 - RHYTHM

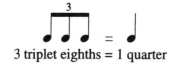

LESSON 45 - PITCH

LESSON 46 - PITCH

LESSON 46 - RHYTHM

LESSON 47 - PITCH

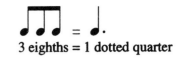

3 eighths = 1 dotted quarter

LESSON 48 - PITCH

LESSON 48 - RHYTHM

LESSON 49 - PITCH

LESSON 49 - RHYTHM

LESSON 50 - PITCH

LESSON 50 - RHYTHM